The King:
Preparing Your Hearts
for Resurrection Sunday

David Benson Kiehn

DEDICATION

To Emmanuel Baptist Church, thank you for allowing me
to experience the power of the King in your midst.

CONTENTS

ACKNOWLEDGMENTS

There are many people to thank for the material in this book. I first want to thank my wife for her faithful and consistent encouragement in my ministry. Her wisdom, daily insights and thoughtful critiques have drastically improved my preaching and thinking. Her impact on my life can simply not be measured.

I also want to thank a number of my brothers and sisters at Park Baptist Church who have helped me think through how to apply biblical principles to a variety of hearers. Park Baptist Church continues to be gracious and kind in how they listen to the Word and strive to apply the Word in every area of their life.

And finally, I want to thank the Sovereign King who came and died and has promised to come again. The Apostle John writes in Rev. 22:20, "He who testifies to these things says, "Surely I am coming soon." Amen. Come, Lord Jesus!"

INTRODUCTION

During membership interviews for our church I always ask people to briefly share the message of the gospel. It usually catches people off guard and makes them a bit nervous, but it is helpful to give people an opportunity to express the truth of the Christian gospel. In all my times asking people to explain the gospel, the number one thing that is left out is the resurrection of Jesus Christ.

It is not that people do not believe in the resurrection, but they usually just leave it out. Paul writes 1 Thess. 4:13-14, "But we do not want you to be uninformed, brothers, about those who are asleep, that you may not grieve as others do who have no hope. For since we believe that Jesus died and rose again, even so, through Jesus, God will bring with him those who have fallen asleep." The resurrection has become more of an afterthought for most Christians. We must be informed.

The resurrection of Christ is the grounds for our Christian hope. Peter writes, "According to his great mercy, he has caused us to be born again to a living hope through the resurrection of Jesus Christ from the dead." Jesus has given us a living hope.

A Living Hope in Our Future Resurrection- Jesus Christ was first fruit of the resurrection. His resurrection gives us hope that one day our lowly bodies will be transformed to be like his glorious body. Death is not our final end, a resurrected glorified body is.

A Living Hope in Our Future Rest – Jesus Christ has promised that in death our race is finished, our battle is done and our rest begins. We no longer have to struggle against this world, the devil and our flesh, but can live in perfect rest with God and His people.

A Living Hope in Our Future Restored Reign – The resurrection is the promise that one day God is going to restore this world back to perfection. The curse will be fully reversed. We will reign in perfect community in a perfect place in God's perfect presence.

The resurrection must never be an afterthought for the Christian. The resurrection is our hope and it is this hope in our future resurrection that should inform all of life.

Beloved, meditate on the resurrection. Consider that we have been born again to a living hope through Christ's resurrection from the dead. Do not be uninformed brothers, one day Jesus Christ will bring us with him to our final resurrected home in our resurrected bodies to live in the resurrected community. So until that day, let us live as citizens of heaven with our hope set on our resurrected home.

I pray this book helps you live in the living hope of the resurrected King as you prepare your hearts for the coming of the King. I pray that your hearts will be full of the joy of the resurrection.

.

CHAPTER 1

THE KING COMES
MATTHEW 21:1-17

In May of 1776, then General George Washington and two others entered the home of a struggling widow seamstress with a design of the first official American flag. Betsy Ross carefully stitched and hemmed the symbol of American freedom. On June 14, 1777, the Continental Congress, hoping to promote unity and national pride, adopted the national flag stating, "Resolved: that the flag of the United States be thirteen stripes, alternate red and white; that the union be thirteen stars, white in a blue field, representing a new constellation.'" The American Flag has grown and changed since Betsy Ross finished her inaugural work, but has continued to stand as a symbol of freedom and national pride for over 200 years.

In 1831 in Salem, Massachusetts Captain William

Driver received an American flag to sail high above his ship, the Charles Doggett. His flag had 24 stars, and as the ship pulled away from the American Coast the crowd could hear him exclaim as he looked high to the ship's mast, "Old Glory!" Driver continued to fly his "Old Glory" when in retirement in Nashville, TN up until the Civil War. When Tennessee seceded from the Union, the confederacy was determined to destroy Driver's famed American flag, but they could not find it. On February 25th, 1862 Union forces captured Nashville and raised a small flag above the capital building. The residents began asking Driver if "Old Glory" still existed. He took a few soldiers back to his residence and started ripping the seams of his bed cover until he finally pulled out the "Old Glory" and made his way back to the Capital. Driver, then 60 years old, climbed up the tower and replaced the small banner with his beloved flag. Driver's devotion to the flag earned all American flags the nickname of "Old Glory.[ii]"

The American flag is a symbol of freedom and national pride. On Palm Sunday, all across America "Old Glory" will be standing and flying to the right of pastors like me as they declare the coming of the King of Glory. What many people do not realize is that placing the flag to the right of the pastor is to give the American Flag the place of honor. According to US Flag Code,

> When displayed with other flags, the size of the
> American Flag should be larger than the other flags or
> relatively equal to the size of the largest flag. Other
> flags should not overshadow the American Flag in any
> way. The American Flag should be flown higher than
> lesser flags. If the flags are displayed on the same level,
> the American Flag should be flown to the (*flag's own*)
> right of all other flags. The right is a position of
> prominence. The flag represents the government of the
> United States, and on American soil, the government is
> the highest authority. The American flag is even
> displayed above church flags.[iii]

In our sanctuary, whether we realize it or not, we are
paying greater honor and giving greater authority to our
earthly ruler than our heavenly one. We live in a great
nation, but the constitution is not more important than the
Bible. We should be patriotic, but our patriotism should
never supersede our devotion to Christ.

On Jesus' triumphal entrance into Jerusalem, we see
the coming of the Messianic King, the One who is worthy
of all our worship. And the coming of Jesus as the King
was a question of authority. Were the people going to
submit to Jesus as their highest authority or continue to

give prominence to their earthly nation? And the amazing thing is that Highest Authority in all the world, comes first not in power, but in humility.

The Humble King Comes

Matthew consistently shows how Jesus fulfills Old Testament prophecies and here is no different,

Now when they drew near to Jerusalem and came to Bethphage, to the Mount of Olives, then Jesus sent two disciples, saying to them, "Go into the village in front of you, and immediately you will find a donkey tied, and a colt with her. Untie them and bring them to me. If anyone says anything to you, you shall say, 'The Lord needs them,' and he will send them at once." This took place to fulfill what was spoken by the prophet, saying, "Say to the daughter of Zion, 'Behold, your king is coming to you, humble, and mounted on a donkey, on a colt, the foal of a beast of burden.'" The disciples went and did as Jesus had directed them. They brought the donkey and the colt and put on them their cloaks, and he sat on them. (Matthew 21:1-6)

Over the last 5 chapters in Matthew's gospel, Jesus was on an intensified mission to get to Jerusalem. He began his

7

journey to Jerusalem with a pronouncement that he must suffer many things from the elders and chief priests and scribes, and be killed.

It was no secret to his disciples why Jesus had entered the heavenly city. Jesus came to die. Jesus came to humble himself to the point of death, even death on a cross (Phil. 2:6-8). The Messianic King had come, but had not come as the people expected. And because Jesus was not the expectation of the people, Matthew highlights how Jesus entered in fulfilment of the messianic prophecy from Zechariah 9:9, verse 4-5,

> This took place to fulfill what was spoken by the prophet, saying, "Say to the daughter of Zion, 'Behold, your king is coming to you, humble, and mounted on a donkey, on a colt, the foal of a beast of burden.'"
> (Matthew 21:4-5)

The Messianic King did not come riding high upon a war horse, but came humble mounted on a donkey. Matthew is showing that Jesus fulfilled the divine prophecy. Jesus is the coming messianic King.

Jesus defied earthly wisdom. He did not come in power, but in humility. If we were in the crowd that day, would we have been excited for humble posture of the coming king? The Jews were living in the holy city under

Roman oppression. They were waiting and longing for the great Messiah to come and to deliver them from foreign rule. The Jews were full of pride for their homeland and were ready for the Messiah to come and bring deliverance. Do you think they would have been satisfied with Jesus' display of humility? Would we? Many of those who filled the crowd were ready to make Israel great again, but did not realize that true greatness comes with humility.

There is no way to known the exact expectations of the people, but we know from the disciples' reaction to the predictions of Jesus death that most of them did not fully realize what was about to happen. Matthew 21:8-11,

> Most of the crowd spread their cloaks on the road, and others cut branches from the trees and spread them on the road. And the crowds that went before him and that followed him were shouting, "Hosanna to the Son of David! Blessed is he who comes in the name of the Lord! Hosanna in the highest!" And when he entered Jerusalem, the whole city was stirred up, saying, "Who is this?" And the crowds said, "This is the prophet Jesus, from Nazareth of Galilee."

Hosanna was a cry of the people for God to save them. They were quoting Psalm 118:25-26 which at the time of the first century was a liturgical hymn of praise for

Yahweh. The people were asking God for salvation, but it was an earthly, nationalistic salvation, not a spiritual one. They were more identified with the earthly kingdom of Israel than spiritual kingdom of Christ.

The whole city was stirred up at the entrance of Jesus. Jesus was used to crowds, but the word for "stirred up" pictures an earthquake implying that Jesus' entrance into Jerusalem sent shockwaves throughout the city. And notice the question that was being asked, "Who is this?" The crowds replied by highlighting how Jesus was the prophet as well as the King. The crowd identifies Jesus with two of the offices of the Old Testament (prophet and King), but the reason Jesus was in Jerusalem was to fulfill the third office of priest. Jesus came to bring salvation to his people through his death as their high priest. Jesus came as the perfect substitute to pay for our sins on the cross. Jesus came in the name of the Lord to offer himself for the salvation of his people. Hebrews 7:26-27,

> For it was indeed fitting that we should have such a high priest, holy, innocent, unstained, separated from sinners, and exalted above the heavens. He has no need, like those high priests, to offer sacrifices daily, first for his own sins and then for those of the people, since he did this once for all when he offered up

himself.

The reason Jesus was in Jerusalem was to humbly offer himself up as the priestly King for his people.

The key is how the people will receive his sacrifice. How will the people answer that question, "Who is this?" The most important question in the world is "who is Jesus?" The question is not merely theological or intellectual question, but it is also an ethical question. It is not enough to rightly identify Jesus as King, but do we live in that reality? Do we live as if Jesus is our highest authority or do we pay him lip service as our king and give prominence to something else?

The crowds were crying out when Jesus entered Jerusalem, "Blessed is he who comes in the name of the Lord!" Jesus quotes this back to the people two chapters later when he is looking over the city. If you would identify yourself as a non-Christian this is particularly important for you to see, Matthew 23:37-39,

"O Jerusalem, Jerusalem, the city that kills the prophets and stones those who are sent to it! How often would I have gathered your children together as a hen gathers her brood under her wings, and you were not willing! See, your house is left to you desolate. For I tell you, you will not see me again, until you say, 'Blessed is he who comes in the name of the Lord.'"

Jesus longs to welcome and gather you as his children as a hen gathers her chicks under her wings. Jesus is willing, but the people are not willing. They did not want to identify Jesus as their Savior and Lord. Jesus tells them how to become his children by repeating back to them what the crowds shouted at his coming, "Blessed is he who comes in the name of the Lord." The people need to identify Jesus as the One who has come from God to save his people through his death and resurrection. Salvation is offered to all, but one must repent of their allegiance to other authorities and place Jesus as their Lord.

My Non-Christian friend, Jesus came to save you. He came to be your King. He came to die on the cross to pay for your sins. The Bible says that all people are sinners and deserving of God's wrath. Jesus came to bring something far better than earthly deliverance. He came to bring eternal deliverance. Jesus entered Jerusalem as the humble King on his way to the cross to be forsaken and rejected so you could be saved. He died and was buried, but God raised him from the dead. He is seated at the right hand of God as the supreme authority over all the earth waiting to bring salvation for all who say, "Blessed is He who comes in the name of the Lord." How you answer the question,

"Who is Jesus?" is the most important question of your life. Jesus wants to be your King, but he wants to be your only King. Turn to Him and be saved.

Beloved, Jesus desires and deserves to be our only and highest allegiance. Notice how Jesus comes to those who claim to be his people, but whose hearts are far from him.

The Zealous King Comes

Jesus is zealous for holiness and true worship. Jesus' harshest rebukes does not come to the world of sinners, but to the religious. Matthew 21:12-13,

> And Jesus entered the temple and drove out all who sold and bought in the temple, and he overturned the tables of the money-changers and the seats of those who sold pigeons. He said to them, "It is written, 'My house shall be called a house of prayer,' but you make it a den of robbers." (Matthew 21:12-13)

Jesus walked into the temple and made a statement. The House of the Lord is run like a business for profit, but should be a house of prayer. Remember how shocking this would have been to the Jewish people. As one scholar notes,

> Who could have expected this sight? The Messiah,

having been led in apparent triumph into the city, enters the temple, arousing expectations of pro-Jewish, nationalist action against Rome. Instead, his attack threatens the sacrificial, worship center of Judaism itself.[iv]

Jesus cares how his people worship. He desires his people to worship him in spirit and in truth. It was time for judgment to begin in the household of God (1 Peter 4:17).

Matthew begins this chapter showing how Jesus fulfills the prophecy in Zechariah. This is significant because of the rest of Zechariah. Ian Campbell draws out this significance when he writes,

By citing Zechariah 9:9 regarding the coming of the King, Matthew draws our attention to this important Old Testament prophet, whose latter prophecies focused on the coming day of the Lord. That day would be a day of salvation (Zech. 9:16). It would also be a day in which 'the glory of the house of David and the glory of the inhabitants of Jerusalem' (Zech. 12:8) would be made great, a day in which the inhabitants of Jerusalem would be cleansed from sin and uncleanness (Zech. 13:1) and in which the people would go to Jerusalem to worship the King (Zech. 14:16). Interestingly, the last statement of Zechariah is that 'there shall no longer be a trader in the house of the Lord of hosts on that day' (Zech. 14:21).[v]

Jesus came to cleanse the temple by ultimately becoming the holy temple for his people. Jesus, the Messianic King, is the One who has authority over the temple and is fulfilling his messianic role to the fullest extent by focusing on the worship of his people.

Jesus has inaugurated his Kingdom on earth. The church is the visible representation of the heavenly kingdom on earth. We are a spiritual outpost as a sign, instrument and foretaste of the kingdom of heaven. Jesus desires our church to reflect him well. We want our church to be fully submitted to the authority of Jesus Christ as our King. Jesus is the head of the Church. He is the Chief Shepherd. His commands and His Word are how we should judge all things pertaining to life and godliness in our community. Our main goal as a church is to make disciples who fully submit to Jesus as King and to grow into fully mature disciples of Christ. And if we make disciples of Jesus who live for his glory then America will change. The goal cannot be a changed America, but if the gospel goes forth in power than America will be changed.

If Jesus walked into our church gathering, what would he say? Would he rebuke or praise our devotion to him? Jesus wrote letters to the churches of the 1st century

15

in Revelation. Jesus speaks to the individual situation of all the churches, but he begins every letter with the words, "I know." Jesus knows our works. He knows how we are loving and not loving each other. He knows if our affections for Him are hot or cold. He knows how we are working for peace or sowing seeds of division. Jesus knows and Jesus cares how we worship. Beloved, let us examine our lives together and make sure that Jesus has the final Word over everything in our life as a church.

The Messianic King Comes

Matthew ends this section of Jesus' entrance into Jerusalem with ministry that is appropriate for the Temple. Matthew 21:14, "And the blind and the lame came to him in the temple, and he healed them." Beloved, there are the spiritually blind and spiritually lame in our world that need the healing of Jesus. We should be a community where our ambition is to offering the healing of the gospel of all who are far from Jesus Christ. And do you know what happens when people get saved and come into our body? Our church changes. Change is inevitable. Change is not easy, but it is inevitable. The challenge for all of us is how do we handle the change in our community in a way that honors the Savior.

The temple community changed. The temple began to be filled with the formerly blind and lame and filled with children all praising God. Matthew 21:15-16,

> But when the chief priests and the scribes saw the wonderful things that he did, and the children crying out in the temple, "Hosanna to the Son of David!" they were indignant, and they said to him, "Do you hear what these are saying?"

The religious leaders were indignant. They were angry and annoyed at the changes in the temple. They were offended at the changes when they should have been praising God. They should have been rejoicing in the salvation ushered in by the long awaited Son of David, but they were focusing on what they were losing rather than what they were gaining. They did not answer the key question of, "Who is this?" correctly. They missed the opportunity to rejoice in the change.

The chief priests and the scribes looked at Jesus with indignation and said, "Do you hear what they are saying?" And Jesus said to them, "Yes; have you never read, "'Out of the mouth of infants and nursing babies you have prepared praise'?" (Matthew 21:16) Jesus highlights Psalm 8 that speaks of the majesty of the Lord in his care for man. God cares for man by sending Jesus to become like a man. Hebrews 2 also quotes Psalm 2 that highlights why the chief priests and the scribes should have been rejoicing, "But we see him who for a little while was made lower than the angels, namely Jesus, crowned with glory and honor because of the suffering of death, so that by the grace of God he might taste death for everyone." (Hebrews 2:9) Jesus has come to taste death for everyone. He has tasted death for the blind and the lame. He has tasted death for the Pharisee and the Scribe. He has tasted death for the religious and the pagan. By the grace of God, Jesus has tasted death for everyone who proclaims and lives, "Blessed is he who comes in the name of the Lord."

Captain William Driver lived his life with the utmost respect and honor to Old glory. He was known by everyone in the town for the respect and honor he gave the flag. Beloved, Jesus is our King. Jesus is our Prophet. Jesus is our Priest. The humble and zealous King came to be our Savior through his death and resurrection. Jesus is the King of Glory. I pray that everyone in our town knows us for how we respect and honor Him who is our Highest Authority. Let us all proclaim and live the truth that, "Blessed is he who comes in the name of the Lord."

CHAPTER 2

THE KING CAME
MARK 10:45

"Why did you come here?" It was a question I was repeatedly asked as I walked through the streets of Maracaibo, Venezuela. I was a tall, burly pale redhead in a land of full of latinos with olive skin and dark hair. I stood out like a sore thumb so I was repeatedly asked, "Why did you come?" Because I looked different and seemed out of place, people wondered what brought me a foreign country. The Eternal Son was out of place in our earthly world. He is perfectly righteous and holy. He was the Eternal God who did not consider equality to be grasped so he made himself nothing, taking the very nature of a servant. What was his purpose? What did Jesus come to the earth?

There could be many possible ways we could answer

these questions, but there are three statements in the gospels that shed light on the what and how of Jesus' ministry on earth. Each verse begins with, "The Son of Man came," allowing us to see his mission and how he fulfilled his mission. As Christians who desire to follow our King it would be wise to pause and reflect on the purpose of His coming so that we can become like Him.

The King Came to Seek and Save

Jesus entered Jericho and met a tax colleting fraud named Zacchaeus. Zacchaeus was befriended by Jesus and who invited himself into Zacchaeus' home for dinner. In the process of that dinner conversation, Zacchaeus repented of his sins and put his faith in Jesus as Lord. The purpose of that encounter is summarized in Luke 19:10, "For the Son of Man came to seek and to save the lost." Jesus was being mocked by the religious elite who grumbled in how he reached out to a fraud. Jesus' kindness did not make sense to the Jews because they did not share the same mission. Jesus came to seek and to save the lost while the Jews wanted to protect and preserve the traditions of their community. Jesus came to reach the frauds, the fakes, and the fools with the power of the gospel.

We all have a story. Our stories are all different, and yet, they are all the same. We all have sinned and we all need a Savior. Jesus Christ came to take your sin upon the cross. He came to seek you and to save you by offering his life for yours. The details of our stories may be different, but the only story of salvation comes through the cross of Christ. Where are you in the story of salvation? Are you like Zacchaeus at the beginning of the story: curious about Christ, yet unsure? Or are you like him at the end of the story, where his joy in Christ caused him to give away his treasured possessions because he had found a better Treasure? Or maybe you are like those grumbling along the way, so focused on yourself that you cannot see how Jesus is seeking those sinners around you? What's your story? Regardless of where you are in your story, know this; Jesus invites you to be part of his story. He is inviting you to join his story of salvation by repenting of your sins and trusting in his life, death and resurrection by faith. Jesus came to seek and to save the lost. We all have our own story, but I pray that you allow His story to become your story.

Jesus' entire life was wrapped up in his mission to bring salvation to the world. If we are going to follow in his steps, then we also must live to seek and to save the lost. Jesus seeks and saves primarily through two ways which are highlighted in the next two statements.

The King Came to Sip and Celebrate

Jesus was always surrounded by controversy. He was followed be fans and skeptics his whole life. People did not know what do to with Jesus as they did not know what to do with John the Baptist. They claimed that John the Baptist had a demon because of his ascetic lifestyle. They claimed that Jesus was to free in his celebrations with tax collectors and sinners. Jesus' ministry was built around the table. It has been said that the gospels show Jesus going to a meal, at a meal or leaving a meal. Matthew 11:19, "The Son of Man came eating and drinking, and they say, 'Look at him! A glutton and a drunkard, a friend of tax collectors and sinners! Yet wisdom is justified by her deeds." Jesus spent time with sinners. How could he seek and save the lost unless he was willing to spend time in their presence?

It is so easy to cloister ourselves into a Christian bubble. Jesus lived his life among the people so that they would be confronted with truth and righteousness through his words and deeds. If we want to recover the heart of

Jesus' ministry, then we must recover his focus on spending time with the lost around the table. It is the simplest of ministries. We all eat. We do not have to add anything new to our schedule, but simply invite people to our table. And we invite people to our table, we are picturing how the Lord has invited us to his table. All of history is moving towards the Great Marriage Supper of the Lamb. On Good Friday, we celebrate the lamb who was slain to take away the sin of the world and that we have the great privilege to offer a foretaste of that Supper as we invite sinners to our table. Jesus shares this parable in Luke 14,

But he said to him, "A man once gave a great banquet and invited many. And at the time for the banquet he sent his servant to say to those who had been invited, 'Come, for everything is now ready.' But they all alike began to make excuses. The first said to him, 'I have bought a field, and I must go out and see it. Please have me excused.' And another said, 'I have bought five yoke of oxen, and I go to examine them. Please have me excused.' And another said, 'I have married a wife, and therefore I cannot come.' So the servant came and reported these things to his master. Then the master of the house became angry and said to his servant, 'Go out quickly to the streets and lanes of the city, and bring in the poor and crippled and blind and lame.' And the servant said, 'Sir, what you commanded has been done, and still there is room.' And the master said to the servant, 'Go out to the highways and hedges and compel people to come in, that my house may be filled. For I tell you, none of those men who were invited shall taste my banquet.'" (Luke 14:16-24)

The cross is our reminder to go out to the highways and hedges and compel people to come in, that God's house may be filled. Jesus came eating and drinking as a foretaste of the kingdom of God.

God wants us to do what He has done for us. We have been invited to the great Marriage Supper of the Lamb. God is preparing a feast and who did he invite? He invited the spiritually poor for theirs is the kingdom of heaven. He invited the spiritually crippled; rise up and walk. He invited the blind; believe and see. God came to us; the spiritually crippled and invited us to his table through his Son. The bible says that because of our sin we are deformed from God's original design. We do not walk upright or see clearly, but rather our hearts our corrupt and even our best offerings are filthy rags in his presence. Sin affects our whole being, therefore it is impossible for us to be right with God. Therefore, God sent Jesus with an invitation. He is the only one who should be invited to the meal because he is the only one without sin. And yet, Jesus gave himself up as our ransom to bring us to God. He died for us so we could have a place at His table. And after he died, God raised him from the dead giving everyone hope for the resurrection to come. Sin has crippled you, but Jesus says I can make you straight. Sin has blinded you, but Jesus says I can make you see. Jesus is willing to heal you, but you must believe in Him. He offers the only real invitation to the Table and that is by faith in his life, death and resurrection. The invitation has been made, will you accept? We accept his invitation by turning from our sin to God. We renounce our pride and self-centeredness and chose to follow Christ in humility. Jesus invites you to the table, have you accepted his invitation?

Jesus offered the invitation to us and now he is sending us out into the world with the same invitation to world. He says, "When you give a dinner or a banquet." He does not say if, but when. We love to eat. We host dinners and parties all the time, but the question is, "who is on our invite list?" Do you only invite those who can pay you back? Do you only invite those that will get you ahead or improve your reputations? Or do you invite the outcasts, the lame, the poor, the crippled, the blind, and the lost?

One of the reasons the American church is dying is because we have forgotten that we were once outcasts, but were brought near through the blood of Christ. We focus on our own health and ignore the spiritually sick that surround us. When we take our eyes off of ourselves and focus on the lost, we will be blessed and be repaid at the resurrection of the just. Do you see how pouring yourselves out to those who can't pay you back, shows that you put your trust in the resurrection of Christ? We give of ourselves to the hurting and the lame, because we know that God will repay us in the resurrection. We offer our homes to the spiritually broken, because God has promised us a place in his home when we were spiritually broken.

Jim Peterson tells the story of friend Mario. Mario was a prideful, Marxist intellectual and loved to read Western philosophers. He was spiritually crippled. After 4 years of reading the Bible together Mario became a Christian. A few years after conversion, Jim and Mario were talking, and Mario asked, "Do you know what it really was that made me decide to become a Christian?" Peterson was sure it would be one of their bible studies or possible a sermon at church, but Mario's answer surprised him. Mario said, "Remember the first time I stopped by your house? We were on our way someplace together, and I had a bowl of soup with you and your family. As I sat there observing you, your wife and your children, and how you related to each other, I asked myself, 'When will I have a relationship like this with my fiancée?' When I realized that the answer was 'never,' I concluded I had to become a Christian for the sake of my own survival. Peterson reflected on the grace of Christ that Mario saw bind that family together:

Our family was unaware of its influence on Mario, God had done this work through our family without knowing it…We tend to see the weaknesses and incongruities in our lives, and our reaction is to recoil at the thought of letting outsiders close enough to see us as we really are. Even if our assessment is accurate, it is my observation that any Christian who is sincerely seeking to walk with God, in spite of all his flaws is reflecting something of Christ.[vi]

Beloved, let us reflect a glimpse of the glory of Christ by inviting the outcasts to our table so they will accept the invitation to God's table.

God invited us to his table when we had nothing to offer. We can never pay back what the Lord has given us. We brought nothing to the table, but sin, unrighteousness, shame and regret. We brought nothing to the table, but have been given everything. Jesus gives us his righteousness, his perfect life, his glory, and his presence. Jesus invites us to his table, let us go and do likewise.

The King Came to Serve and Sacrifice

Jesus came to seek and to save the lost and He sought the lost by inviting people to fellowship with him around the table, but it would all have been for nothing if he did not finish his atoning work in becoming our ransom. The key verse in Mark's Gospel is Mark 10:45, "For even the Son of Man came not to be served but to serve, and give his life as a ransom for many." Jesus came to serve and give his life as a ransom. The Eternal Son, the Creator of the Universe, the Prince of Peace, the King of Glory, the immortal God humbled himself by taking on the very nature of a servant being made in human likeness. God became our Passover Lamb who was slain to take away our sins.

Christians celebrate Jesus on Good Friday, but the only way we can truly celebrate is to first meditate on our own sin. We deserve to die. We deserve to be punished for our iniquity. We deserve to be crushed for our sin and rebellion. How many times have we harbored bitterness

28

against others and grumbled in discontentment? How many times have we loved worldly things over God and neglected our true purpose in life? How many times have we deliberately sinned? My list is long. And if you are honest, so is yours. God is so holy and righteous that to spurn his grace deserves nothing but his furious wrath. It is a fearful thing to fall into the hands of the living God. (Hebrews 10:31) We will never appreciate Good Friday unless we understand the gross nature of our sin and the just punishment it deserves. Allow the weight of our rightly deserved punishment to weigh down our souls. Take a whole minute just to think of your sin.

And now think that Jesus gave his life for it all. Jesus became our ransom. His blood was shed. His body was crushed. He was forsaken and smitten by God. And he did it willing: *for the joy that was set before him he endured the cross; for our sake, he became sin who knew no sin.*

And can it be that I should gain

An interest in the Savior's blood?

Died He for me, who caused His pain—

For me, who Him to death pursued?

Amazing love! How can it be,

That Thou, my God, shouldst die for me?

Amazing love! How can it be,

That Thou, my God, shouldst die for me?

He died for you. Does the death of Christ amaze you? We never outgrow our need of hearing the beauty and majesty of the death of Christ for sinners. Jesus paid our ransom.

In his book <u>Written In Blood</u>, Robert Coleman tells the story of a little boy whose sister needed a blood transfusion, he writes,

> The doctor explained that she had the same disease the boy had recovered from two years earlier. Her only chance for recovery was a transfusion from someone who had previously conquered the disease. Since the two children had the same rare blood type, the boy was the ideal donor.
>
> "Would you give your blood to Mary?" the doctor asked. Johnny hesitated. His lower lip started to tremble. Then he smiled and said, "Sure, for my sister." Soon the two children were wheeled into the hospital room--Mary, pale and thin; Johnny, robust and healthy. Neither spoke, but when their eyes met, Johnny grinned. As the nurse inserted the needle into his arm, Johnny's smile faded. He watched the blood flow through the tube.
>
> With the ordeal almost over, his voice, slightly shaky,

broke the silence. "Doctor, when do I die?'

Only then did the doctor realize why Johnny had hesitated, why his lip had trembled when he'd agreed to donate his blood. He's thought giving his blood to his sister meant giving up his life.[vii]

Johnny was willing to die to save the life of his sister. Fortunately, Johnny did not have to die, but our condition is far worse. Our sinful condition required Jesus to give not only his blood, but his life as our ransom. Johnny did it for his sister, Jesus did it for sinners.

Jesus freely offers his life to all, but notice Mark 10:45 says that Jesus came to give his life as a ransom for many. Jesus offered his life to all, but his ransom was only paid for those who repent of their sin and trust in Christ. Jesus offers his life to all, but his death is only effective for those who receive him as a Lord and Savior. Jesus is our Savior because he died for us and our Lord because he was raised from the dead and now sits at the right hand of God Most High. Have you placed all your hope for forgiveness and acceptance of God in the death of Christ on your behalf? Is Jesus your ransom? Are you one of the many who will trust Him or one of those who turn away?

We gather today as God's people to remember and rejoice in the death of Christ for our sake. Jesus came to serve and sacrifice himself for his people. "He himself bore our sins in his body on the tree, that we might die to sin and live to righteousness. By his wounds you have been healed." (1 Peter 2:24) Beloved, tonight, we come to the feast, we come to the table, the great and the least, the rich and the poor, only because Christ is our ransom. The cross of Jesus Christ declares us guilty of sin, but it also demonstrates God's immense love for us that while we were yet sinners, Christ died for us. Beloved, let us come to the table remembering Christ our Ransom. He came to seek and to save sinners, like you and me, by serving them in giving his life as our sacrifice, our Ransom.

CHAPTER 3

THE KING WILL COME
MARK 16:1-8

There is nothing more terrifying than the feeling of when your child is lost. When I was 4 years old my family lived in Cedar Rapids, IA. One night we came home from dinner with friends and my parents heard a car skid out in the neighborhood and looked to the street just in time to see the car speed off. It was an unusual event in our quiet neighborhood so naturally parents started to make sure that all their children were accounted for. My parents looked all around, but could not find me. Their hearts sunk and all they could think of was the worst possible scenario that their baby boy was kidnapped by that car that skidded and speed off in that quiet neighborhood. They woke up the neighbors and canvassed the entire area for two hours.

Can you imagine the fear that filled the hearts of my parents? The dread and the panic that gripped their thoughts. If you ever lost a child even for a few moments, you have a small understanding what my parents were filling that night. After a two-hour search, one of my neighbors went back into the garage lifted up a big green garbage bucket and found me asleep under it. To this day, I have no recollection why on earth I felt the need to put a garbage bucket over my head to sleep, but I did. A day that started out horrible turned into one of our favorite family stories. "Hey remember when Dave feel asleep in the garbage bucket!!" A night full of fear ended with incredible joy.

Can you imagine the fear and the pain of the disciples? They walked with Jesus for three years. They ate together and served together. They put all their hope into him to deliver the nation of Israel. Their mighty leader brutally condemned and crucified. The eyes of the world, Jesus was cursed, "for it is written, 'Cursed is everyone who is hanged on a tree.'" Those disciples experience the worst Sabbath of their lives. It was full of fear and the unknown. And we begin Mark's account of the Resurrection with, "When the Sabbath was past." It was a Sabbath of fear and dread, but that terrible night will become the best story ever. A night full of dread will become the favorite story of all the world.

I do not know the fears and anxiety that you bring with you today. It could be fear over financial stress and the anxiety of how the bills are going to be paid. It could be fear over the direction of your children's life and the anxiety that fills the heart wondering if they are ever going to turn it around. It could be fear over a friend's faith and the anxiety of watching those you love make poor choices. Whatever fears you bring here today, I know that the resurrection of Jesus Christ can calm those fears.

The Resurrected King Calms Fear

One of the greatest signs of the veracity of the resurrection account is that all of the gospels give a prominent place to women as the first witnesses of the resurrection of Christ. In the first century, women would not have been ideal choices to fabricate a story because they were not looked as reliable witnesses. They were not even allowed to testify in court. Notice how Mark highlights the role of women of the discovery of the resurrection. Mark 16:1-3,

> When the Sabbath was past, Mary Magdalene, Mary the mother of James, and Salome bought spices, so that they might go and anoint him. And very early on the

first day of the week, when the sun had risen, they went to the tomb. And they were saying to one another, "Who will roll away the stone for us from the entrance of the tomb?"

These women were going to anoint the body of Jesus. They were expecting Jesus' body to be there. They were prepared to see Jesus. Even though Jesus had told the disciples that after his death, he was going to be raised from the dead, the expectations of the women, and most likely the men, was that Jesus was going to be in the tomb. The women had brought spices and were concerned how the stone was going to be moved so that they were able to anoint Jesus' body.

Some of the greatest witnesses of the power of God are those who were not expecting to see the power of God. The women were not ready to see the resurrection, but they were the ones who first witness it, Mark 16:4-7,

And looking up, they saw that the stone had been rolled back—it was very large. And entering the tomb, they saw a young man sitting on the right side, dressed in a white robe, and they were alarmed. And he said to them, "Do not be alarmed. You seek Jesus of Nazareth, who was crucified. He has risen; he is not here. See the place where they laid him. But go, tell his disciples and Peter that he is going before you to

Galilee. There you will see him, just as he told you."
(Mark 16:4-7)

As they approached the tomb, the large stone was rolled away. They entered the tomb and turned to the right where the body should have been laid, but instead saw a man dressed in white robe. Mark is implying that the women saw an angel of the Lord with his description. All angels in the Bible are classified as men. This angel sees that these were alarmed.

The Greek word for alarmed here is common in Mark's gospel. Mark uses it both as amazement or as terror. The translated here decided to translate this word 'alarmed.' I think there would have been a mixture of both amazement and terror as those women entered the tomb. They were expecting to see Jesus, but he was gone. The angel saw their fear whether by divine revelation or by observing their fear on their faces, and said, "Do not be alarmed." The angel calmed their fears by sharing the truth of the resurrection. The truth of the resurrection should always calm our fears. Whether we are just beginning to inquire of Jesus Christ or whether we have been lifelong believers, hearing of the resurrection of Jesus Christ should calm all our fears.

The angel uses a very specific title for Jesus. He says, "You seek Jesus of Nazareth, who was crucified. He has risen; he is not here." Mark draws out the historical Jesus Christ. There are some who claim that Jesus' resurrection was not a bodily resurrection, but merely a spiritual resurrection. In a society that is growing increasingly secular, the idea that a man could be raised from the dead to life is too hard to grasp. The New Testament does not explain the resurrection in spiritual terms, but explain the resurrection of Jesus Christ as an event of history. The man Jesus from Nazareth, Mary's son, who grew up in the region of Galilee of Judea, who was actually crucified on a real Roman cross on a literal day in history, Jesus of Nazareth, has risen. It is important to note that the New Testament teaches a literal bodily resurrection of Jesus Christ. We should accept the historical record of the Bible explaining a real event in History.

When Paul wrote to the church of Corinth, he passed his entire life on the literal bodily resurrection of Jesus Christ. 1 Corinthians 15:12-21,

> Now if Christ is proclaimed as raised from the dead, how can some of you say that there is no resurrection of the dead? But if there is no resurrection of the dead, then not even Christ has been raised. And if Christ has not been raised, then our preaching is in vain and your faith is in vain. We are even found to be misrepresenting God, because we testified about God

that he raised Christ, whom he did not raise if it is true that the dead are not raised. For if the dead are not raised, not even Christ has been raised. And if Christ has not been raised, your faith is futile and you are still in your sins. Then those also who have fallen asleep in Christ have perished. If in Christ we have hope in this life only, we are of all people most to be pitied. But in fact Christ has been raised from the dead, the firstfruits of those who have fallen asleep. For as by a man came death, by a man has come also the resurrection of the dead.

The resurrection of Jesus should calm our fears because Jesus was the firstfruits of those who had fallen asleep. Paul says that as through Adam came death, by the man, Jesus of Nazareth will come the resurrection of the dead.

Humans fear death. The desire for survival is the greatest of human instincts. The resurrection of Jesus Christ should calm our fears because it solves are greatest problem. Through Adam's sin, death came into the world. Romans 5:12, "Therefore, just as sin came into the world through one man, and death through sin, and so death spread to all men because all sinned." All human beings desire to survive because they know in the deepest part of their hearts that upon death they will face judgment for their sin. We cannot escape the fear of death because we know that we are going to meet God. Jesus came to die in our place on the cross. He came to take our judgment on the tree to be cursed for us. Mark 10:45, "For even the Son of Man came not to be served but to serve, and to give his life as a ransom for many." The only way for Jesus to die in our place was that if he was a sinless, perfect man. For our sake, he who knew no sin, became sin for us. But we rejoice in the resurrection for as Jesus literally took our punishment on the cross, he literally rose from the dead as our justification.

The resurrection of Jesus Christ is God's stamp of approval on his sacrifice. Mark uses the Divine passive in Mark 16:6 implying that it was God that raised Jesus from the dead. God raised Jesus to calm the fears of the world by giving them the hope of the resurrection. If you have not trusted in Christ as your Lord and Savior, the resurrection is your invitation to turn from your fear of death and put your hope in Jesus Christ. God approved of Jesus' sacrifice and now he is asking you to turn from your sins and receive his mercy so that you can be born again to a living hope through Jesus Christ from the dead to an inheritance that is undefiled, imperishable and unfading kept in heaven for us through faith in Him. Will you heed the words of the angel spoken to those women so many years go, "Do not be alarmed. He has risen."

The women should not have expected Jesus to be in the tomb. Notice the last words of the angel, "But go, tell his disciples and Peter that he is going before you to Galilee. There you will see him, *just as he told you.*" (Mark 16:7) The women lived in fear because they did not trust the words of Jesus. Friend, allow Jesus to calm your fears by trusting in his words. Believe in his resurrection.

The Resurrected King Creates Fear

It seems like a contradiction to say that the resurrection calms fear, but also creates fear. Although it seems like a contradiction, that was the response of the women at the end of Mark's gospel, Mark 16:8, "And they went out and fled from the tomb, for trembling and astonishment had seized them, and they said nothing to anyone, for they were afraid." The earliest Greek manuscripts do not include Mark 16:9-20. It is believed that someone came an added the last section of Mark's gospel because it appeared that ending was too abrupt. It did not make sense to the earliest Christians that Mark's gospel would have ended with the women being afraid.

Scholar James Brooks, provides three reasons why he believes that Mark's gospel ends so abruptly and is fitting with the rest of the book,

41

First an ending with references to trembling, bewilderment, flight, and fear is not surprising or out of place as many have thought because Mark previously recorded similar reactions when people observed the power of God being manifested in Jesus. (All throughout Mark's Gospel, people respond to God's power with fear and amazement.)

Second, the abrupt ending is quite in harmony with the abrupt beginning of the Gospel. Just as Mark recorded very little that preceded the ministry of Jesus, so he recorded very little that followed it.

Third, Mark had a definite purpose in his ending. He apparently wanted an open ending to indicate that the story was not complete but was continuing beyond the time he wrote. He wanted his readers/hearers to continue the story in their own lives. By stating that the women told no one, he challenged his readers/hearers to assume the responsibility of telling the good news to everyone.[viii]

I especially appreciate his last observation. Christianity does not end with hearing about the resurrection, but with Christians going and sharing what they have seen and heard.

How said would it be for Christians to say nothing of the resurrection? We may look negatively at Mark's ending or at the women who were afraid, but how often are we in the same situation. The resurrection creates fear in us because it forces us to be at odds with our world. The resurrection forces us to confront a naturalistic, anti-miracle worldview when we tell people that we actually believe that Jesus rose from the dead. How many times have we had the opportunity to share the greatest story ever told with a lost friend or neighbor, but have remained silent because of our fear of rejection? Do you believe in the resurrection? If you believe, why would you not share it? How could Christians keep silent?

Beloved, if the resurrection is true it puts us at odds with the world. The death, burial and resurrection of Jesus Christ provides a distinct way of viewing the world. Are we going to be overcome with fear or all the power of the resurrection to conquer our fears?

The Resurrected King Conquers Fear

The Gospel of Mark ends in fear, but we have the book of Acts. We have the rest of the story how disciples of Jesus Christ have become witnesses of the resurrection in Jerusalem, Judea, Samaria and the ends of the earth. We are a product of the how the resurrected King conquered the fear of the disciples. Peter and John were confronted by the Sanhedrin for a miracle done to a crippled man. Acts 4:13, "Now when they saw the boldness of Peter and John, and perceived that they were uneducated, common men, they were astonished. And they recognized that they had been with Jesus." Peter and John conquered their fears of death and rejection because they had spent time with Jesus. They believed in the resurrection and it changed their life.

Have you ever stood on top of a mountain? It is incredible sight to look down on everything below knowing that there is nothing above and nothing higher than where you stand. Standing on the top of a mountain is so sweet because we know of the labor and physical exertion that was necessary to reach the top for mountaintops cannot be reached without a struggle.

Jesus Christ is now seated on the supreme mountaintop of His own glory. He is far above all rule and authority and power and dominion and above every name that is named, not only in this age but also in the one to come. There is no one above our Sovereign Lord. He sits at the right hand of God with full authority and power until all His enemies are made His footstool. The resurrected King conquers are fears because he has been exalted to the highest place and been given the names above all names. And yet, the only way Jesus was exalted to the highest place was because of

His willingness to walk up Calvary's hill in obedience to the Father. Phil 2:8-11,

> And being found in human form, he humbled himself by becoming obedient to the point of death, *even death on a cross. Therefore God has highly exalted him* and bestowed on him the name that is above every name, so that at the name of Jesus every knee should bow, in heaven and on earth and under the earth, and every tongue confess that Jesus Christ is Lord, to the glory of God the Father.

It is only in Christ's giving of Himself in death that He was exalted to the highest place. And because Christ is seated on the throne, we as His people know that nothing can separate us from his love. He is the one who died and who was raised. And knowing that our God is far above all authority and power gives us the freedom to follow Christ in giving ourselves in humiliation so that one day we will be exalted (1 Peter 5:6).

Beloved, our great and glorious Savior is seated at the right hand of God as the supreme authority over all else. And this all powerful Savior always stands before the Father interceding for us as our High Priest. He is our King and our Priest. His death and resurrection secure for us an eternal hope through faith. We have nothing to fear for He who is supreme is the One who speaks for us.

One Day our King will come again. And on that Day it will be clear that we have no reason to fear. Acts 17:31, "because he has fixed a day on which he will judge the world in righteousness by a man whom he has appointed; and of this he has given assurance to all by raising him from the dead." The resurrection is our assurance that Jesus will come again. We do not need to fear, because Jesus has conquered our fears. Revelation 21:5-7,

> And he who was seated on the throne said, "Behold, I am making all things new." Also he said, "Write this down, for these words are trustworthy and true." And he said to me, "It is done! I am the Alpha and the Omega, the beginning and the end. To the thirsty I will give from the spring of the water of life without payment. The one who conquers will have this heritage, and I will be his God and he will be my son.

The one who conquers will have this heritage, that God will be our God and that we will be his children. Beloved, we conquer our fears by believing in the resurrection of Jesus Christ from the dead who conquered the grave on our behalf. The One who is seated on the throne will come again.

He was lifted up to die;
"It is finished" was his cry;
now in heaven exalted high:

Hallelujah, what a Savior!
When he comes, our glorious King,
all his ransomed home to bring,
then anew this song we'll sing:
Hallelujah, what a Savior!

Beloved, our glorious King is coming. Let us live as conquerors by trusting in our Conquering King. Hallelujah, what a Savior!

CONCLUSION

THE JOY OF THE RESURRECTED KING

Men have searched long and far for joy. Interestingly, those who have accomplished the greatest worldly glory found that joy escaped them.

Joy cannot be found in Unbelief -- for the famous atheist philosopher Voltaire was an infidel of the most pronounced type. He wrote: "I wish I had never been born."

Joy cannot be found in Pleasure -- Lord Byron lived a life of pleasure only to end up empty, when he wrote: "The worm, the canker, and grief are mine alone."

Joy cannot be found in Money -- Jay Gould, the American millionaire, when dying, he said: "I suppose I am the most miserable man on earth."

Joy cannot be found in Position and Fame – Famous English politician Lord Beaconsfield enjoyed them both, he sadly wrote: "Youth is a mistake; manhood a struggle; old age a regret."

Joy cannot be found in Military Glory -- Alexander the Great
conquered the known world in his day. Having done
so, he wept in his tent, before he said, "There are no
more worlds to conquer."ix

Jesus birth brought great joy to the people. Luke 2:10-11,
"And the angel said to them, "Fear not, for behold, I bring
you good news of great joy that will be for all the people.
For unto you is born this day in the city of David a Savior,
who is Christ the Lord." As Jesus birth brought great joy,
his death brought great sorrow. The disciples wept at his
death and burial. Things seems all but lost until God gave
Jesus a rebirth and victory over the grave. God restored
joy to all people in the resurrection of Christ. The
resurrection is the foundation of true joy. True and lasting
joy can only be found the resurrection of Jesus Christ from
the dead.

The early church new of great persecution, but they
also knew of glorious joy. I have been reminded more and
more of late of the importance of the joy of believers. I
asked a group of college students recently what is the first
thing they look for when they walk into a church. The
answers varied from the people's appearance, to the style
of music, the reverence of the word, but I think one of the
things that should be evident in the life of a church is joy.
Does joy permeate our body? Do people get a sense of the

joy that we have in Christ?

The disciples in the book of Acts were called to be witnesses for Jesus Christ. They were given the Holy Spirit and were sent to be witnesses in Jerusalem, Judea, Samaria and to the ends of the earth. And where they went as witnesses of the risen Christ, they went with joy because they had received forgiveness of sin and salvation through Christ. I pray this chapter you will see ways we can have joy in the resurrected Christ.

The Joy in the Preaching the Resurrected King

Stephen was the first Christian martyr. After he confessed that Jesus was the Christ, he was brutally stoned to death. After Stephen's death, it was clear to all Christians throughout Jerusalem that to stand for Jesus was to put oneself in grave danger. Led by Saul of Tarsus, a great persecution arose against the church in Jerusalem causing God's people to scatter. Acts 8:3, "But Saul was ravaging the church, and entering house after house, he dragged off men and women and committed them to prison." As Christian friends and neighbors were being carted off to prison because of their faith, one would think that this effectively squash the Christian movement, but instead it only strengthened it.

50

The gospel has always advanced in the face of persecution. It advances because Christians are so full of joy that they can't stop sharing the message of Christ. Act 8:4-5, "Now those who were scattered went about preaching the word. Philip went down to the city of Samaria and proclaimed to them the Christ." (Acts 8:4-5) All the disciples except the Apostles fled Jerusalem preaching the word. After Stephen's death, they now know the great lengths that the Jews are willing to go to silence them from sharing the resurrected Christ, but they just keep sharing. They shared Christ because they were full of joy of the resurrection. Jesus Christ had risen from the dead. He was alive seated at the right hand of God. He gave them victory over death and the grave. He freed them for the power and bondage to sin. They could not stop sharing of the resurrection.

God's people should be full of joy as they preach about the resurrected Christ. What a great privilege it is to share Christ. Jesus died and was raised to give new life to the lost. He came to seek and to save the lost by dying in their place and being raised from the dead. Everyone who was scattered from Jerusalem preached the gospel. It was not only for the ordained, trained clergy, but it was for all believers in Christ. All Christians have been entrusted with the gospel and empowered with the Holy Spirit of God.

We all must find joy in preaching the resurrected Christ.

The average American Christian shares the gospel zero times every year. If we had the joy of the resurrection, it would not be possible for us to be silent. Star Wars Episode 7 came out in November and everyone was talking about how great the movie was for weeks. Batman vs. Superman came out this past week and thousands of lifelong fans are posting and tweeting about its greatness. Be happy about Star Wars, Batman and Superman, but be full joy of the resurrection of Christ. Jesus rose from the dead. And if we believe in Christ as our Lord and Savior, we will one day be raise from the dead. "For if we have been united with him in a death like his, we shall certainly be united with him in a resurrection like his." (Romans 6:5)

If we have not found joy in sharing the gospel this past year, we may not to study more about the resurrection of Christ. The Lord has given us a weekly rhythm so that we would never forget the resurrection. Every Sunday is the Lord's Day. The Lord's Day is on Sunday because it reminds us of the resurrection of Jesus from the dead. The weekly reminder of God's goodness to us in Christ should fuel our joy throughout the week as we go like Philip proclaiming that Jesus is the Christ throughout our city.

The Joy in the Power of Resurrected King

The resurrection fuels our joy in our preaching, because we see its power in people lives. Acts 8:6-7, "And the crowds with one accord paid attention to what was being said by Philip when they heard him and saw the signs that he did. For unclean spirits, crying out with a loud voice, came out of many who had them, and many who were paralyzed or lame were healed." The gospel changes lives. The gospel changes lives because of the resurrection power of the Spirit of God. Romans 8:11, "If the Spirit of him who raised Jesus from the dead dwells in you, he who raised Christ Jesus from the dead will also give life to your mortal bodies through his Spirit who dwells in you." The Spirit that gave the resurrection to Christ dwells in you Christian. The Spirit of God will give life through your mortal body.

The Spirit of God will make the lame healed and the paralyzed walk. The Spirit that brought Christ resurrection from the dead will also bring about resurrection from those who are spiritually dead. This past week my son said, "I don't see many miracles." My wife responded by saying miracles are rare. Miracles are rarer than we want, because we too often limit the power of God. We do not believe that God has the power to transform sinners into saints.

After incidents like Brussels and the Ivory Coast this past week, our hearts are screaming out for justice. We want justice for those who were slain, but we should also continue to preached the One who was slain that has the power to change lives. The gospel is stronger enough to save a terrorist. Even in this very chapter of Scripture we see a terrorist ravaging the church going from house to house to root out and punish all believers of Christ. And that terrorist saw the resurrected Christ and became the greatest missionary in the history of Christianity. The gospel is powerful for it comes with the resurrection power of the Spirit of God.

Do we have joy in the resurrected power of Jesus Christ? Do we believe that Jesus can still change lives by his Spirit? People saw the signs of Philip and saw the changed lives and they listen to the word of God. The greatest testimony to the lost is a changed life. Have you experienced the joy? John Newton was a former slave owner. He repented and believed in the resurrected Christ and gave the rest of his life to stop the slave trade. He wrote, "I am not what I ought to be, I am not what I want to be, I am not what I hope to be in another world; but still I am not what I once used to be, and by the grace of God I am what I am." By the grace of God, you have been changed. Let us continue to strive to live by the power of the resurrection. Paul wrote,

Indeed, I count everything as loss because of the surpassing worth of knowing Christ Jesus my Lord. For his sake I have suffered the loss of all things and count them as rubbish, in order that I may gain Christ and be found in him, not having a righteousness of my own that comes from the law, but that which comes through faith in Christ, the righteousness from God that depends on faith—that I may know him and the power of his resurrection, and may share his sufferings, becoming like him in his death, that by any means possible I may attain the resurrection from the dead. Not that I have already obtained this or am already perfect, but I press on to make it my own, because Christ Jesus has made me his own. Brothers, I do not consider that I have made it my own. But one thing I do: forgetting what lies behind and straining forward to what lies ahead, I press on toward the goal for the prize of the upward call of God in Christ Jesus. (Philippians 3:8-14)

We are not what we want to be, but thanks be to God we are not what we used to be. Brothers, forget what is behind and press on toward the goal of the resurrection of the upward call of God in Christ Jesus.

The Joy of the People of Resurrected King

The last line of this paragraph is a beautiful goal for our city. Acts 8:8, "So there was much joy in that city." What a great goal and ambition for out church. We can live in the joy of the resurrection so that others may know that joy. Just imagine a city what was full of joy because it had experienced the preaching and the power of the resurrection. It is an anticipated conclusion that God's people would be full of joy. We are a people of the resurrection. There should not be a more joyful place in the world than the local church. That does not mean that we are always happy, for joy transcend happiness. Job had lost everything. His home, his children and his wealth and after he had lost it all he said, "Naked I came from my mother's womb, and naked shall I return. The LORD gave, and the LORD has taken away; blessed be the name of the LORD." (Job 1:21). Blessed be the name of the LORD!! Joy transcend happiness.

Our goal is not to transform society, but to transform people who will transform society. If we all live in the joy of the resurrected Christ, our joy will spill over to our society. Think of the joy that could be in your neighborhoods, your workplaces, and your homes, if we live in that joy? Beloved, let us make it our ambition to have joy in our city. Walk in the joy of the resurrection. Share the joy of the resurrection. Rejoice as you watch others experience that joy. And pray for the joy of the resurrection to permeate our city.

OTHER TITLES by
Pastor David Kiehn

THE LORD CALLS SINNERS

GUARD YOUR SOULS

A FORGIVING FRIEND

THE CHURCH: THE HOUSEHOLD OF THE LIVING GOD

QUESTIONING THE MINOR PROPHETS

THE WISDOM OF PROVERBS

ABOUT THE AUTHOR

Dave Kiehn is the Senior Pastor of the Park Baptist Church in Rock Hill, SC. He graduated with a B.A. in Intellectual History from the University of Pennsylvania and received his Masters of Divinity at Southeastern Baptist Theological Seminary. Pastor Kiehn is currently pursuing his PhD at Southeastern in North American Missiology. He has authored several books. He is married to his beautiful wife, Ellen, and they have three children, Elizabeth, John David and Olivia.

End Notes

[i] http://www.ushistory.org/betsy/flagtale.html accessed 3.19.2016

[ii] http://www.usflag.org/old.glory.story.html accessed 3.19.2016

[iii] http://www.united-states-flag.com/displaying-flags.html accessed 3.19.2016

[iv] Blomberg, C. (1992). *Matthew* (Vol. 22, p. 314). Nashville: Broadman & Holman Publishers.

[v] Campbell, I. D. (2008). *Opening up Matthew* (p. 131). Leominster: Day One Publications.

[vi] Cheter, Tim. A Meal with Jesus: Discovering Grace, Community and Mission Around the Table. Crossway. Wheaton, Il. p.94-95 2011.

[vii] http://www.sermonillustrations.com/a-z/a/atonement.htm accessed 3.25.16

[viii] Brooks, J. A. (1991). *Mark* (Vol. 23, p. 275). Nashville: Broadman & Holman Publishers.

[ix] *The Bible Friend*, Turning Point, May, 1993.

www.ingramcontent.com/pod-product-compliance
Lightning Source LLC
Chambersburg PA
CBHW060711030426
42337CB00017B/2835